This Recipe Book belongs to:

 # Table of Contents 

Table of Contents

Table of Contents

Table of Contents

Table of Contents

Table of Contents

Table of Contents

EATING IS A *necessity* BUT COOKING *is an art.*

Name:

Date: .... Source: ....

○ Starter ○ Main Course ○ Dessert ○ Baking

Servings: .... Prep Time: .... Cook Time: ....

Difficulty: ○ ○ ○ ○ ○

Ingredients

....

....

....

....

....

....

....

....

....

Personal Notes:

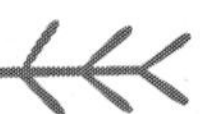

Directions:

....

....

....

....

....

....

....

....

....

....

Rating:

Personal Notes:

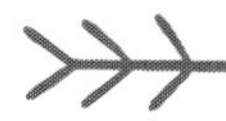

2 Name:

Date: ....   Source: ....

◯ Starter   ◯ Main Course   ◯ Dessert   ◯ Baking

Servings: ....   Prep Time: ....   Cook Time: ....

Difficulty: ◯   ◯   ◯   ◯   ◯

Ingredients

....

....

....

....

....

....

....

....

....

Personal Notes:

Directions:

Rating: 🧑‍🍳 🧑‍🍳 🧑‍🍳 🧑‍🍳 🧑‍🍳

Personal Notes:

3 Name:

Date: .... Source: ....

○ Starter   ○ Main Course   ○ Dessert   ○ Baking

Servings: ....   Prep Time: ....   Cook Time: ....

Difficulty: ○   ○   ○   ○   ○

Ingredients

....

....

....

....

....

....

....

....

....

Personal Notes:

Directions:

Rating: 

Personal Notes:

4 Name:
....

Date: .... Source: ....

○ Starter ○ Main Course ○ Dessert ○ Baking

Servings: .... Prep Time: .... Cook Time: ....

Difficulty: ○ ○ ○ ○ ○

Ingredients

....

....

....

....

....

....

....

....

....

Personal Notes:

Directions:

Rating:

Personal Notes:

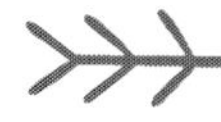

19

5 Name:

Date: Source:

○ Starter   ○ Main Course   ○ Dessert   ○ Baking

Servings: Prep Time: Cook Time:

Difficulty: ○ ○ ○ ○ ○

Ingredients

Personal Notes:

Directions:

Rating: 🔲🔲🔲🔲🔲

Personal Notes:

6 Name:

Date: Source:

○ Starter   ○ Main Course   ○ Dessert   ○ Baking

Servings: Prep Time: Cook Time:

Difficulty: ○   ○   ○   ○   ○

Ingredients

Personal Notes:

Directions:

Rating: 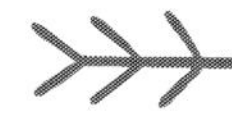

Personal Notes:

Name:

Date: .... Source: ....

○ Starter   ○ Main Course   ○ Dessert   ○ Baking

Servings: .... Prep Time: .... Cook Time: ....

Difficulty: ○   ○   ○   ○   ○

Ingredients

....

....

....

....

....

....

....

....

....

Personal Notes:

Directions:

....

....

....

....

....

....

....

....

....

....

Rating: 

Personal Notes:

8

Name:

Date: .... Source: ....

◯ Starter   ◯ Main Course   ◯ Dessert   ◯ Baking

Servings: ....   Prep Time: ....   Cook Time: ....

Difficulty: ◯   ◯   ◯   ◯   ◯

Ingredients

....

....

....

....

....

....

....

....

....

Personal Notes:

Directions:

Rating: 

Personal Notes:

9 Name:

Date: .... Source: ....

○ Starter ○ Main Course ○ Dessert ○ Baking

Servings: .... Prep Time: .... Cook Time: ....

Difficulty: ○ ○ ○ ○ ○

Ingredients

....

....

....

....

....

....

....

....

....

Personal Notes:

Directions:

....

....

....

....

....

....

....

....

....

....

Rating:

Personal Notes:

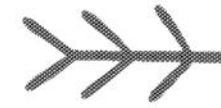

10 Name:

Date: Source:

○ Starter   ○ Main Course   ○ Dessert   ○ Baking

Servings: Prep Time: Cook Time:

Difficulty: ○   ○   ○   ○   ○

Ingredients

Personal Notes:

Directions:

Rating: 

Personal Notes:

Name:
....

Date: .... Source: ....

○ Starter   ○ Main Course   ○ Dessert   ○ Baking

Servings: .... Prep Time: .... Cook Time: ....

Difficulty: ○   ○   ○   ○   ○

Ingredients

....

....

....

....

....

....

....

....

....

Personal Notes:

Directions:

....

....

....

....

....

....

....

....

....

....

Rating:

Personal Notes:

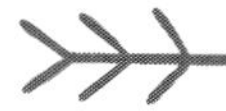

12 Name:

Date: .... Source: ....

○ Starter   ○ Main Course   ○ Dessert   ○ Baking

Servings: ....   Prep Time: ....   Cook Time: ....

Difficulty: ○ ○ ○ ○ ○

Ingredients

....

....

....

....

....

....

....

....

Personal Notes:

Directions:

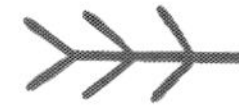

Rating:

Personal Notes:

13 Name:

Date: Source:

○ Starter ○ Main Course ○ Dessert ○ Baking

Servings: _____ Prep Time: _____ Cook Time: _____

Difficulty: ○ ○ ○ ○ ○

Ingredients

Personal Notes:

Directions:

Rating:

Personal Notes:

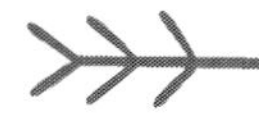 

14 **Name:**
....

Date: .... Source: ....

○ Starter   ○ Main Course   ○ Dessert   ○ Baking

Servings: .... Prep Time: .... Cook Time: ....

Difficulty: ○   ○   ○   ○   ○

Ingredients

....

....

....

....

....

....

....

....

....

Personal Notes:

Directions:

Rating:

Personal Notes:

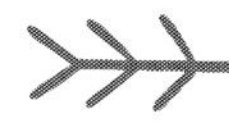

39

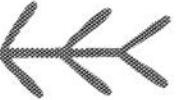

15 Name:

Date:

Source:

○ Starter ○ Main Course ○ Dessert ○ Baking

Servings: Prep Time: Cook Time:

Difficulty: ○ ○ ○ ○ ○

Ingredients

Personal Notes:

Directions:

Rating: 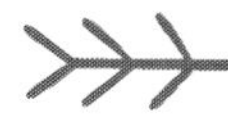

Personal Notes:

16 Name:

Date: .... Source: ....

○ Starter   ○ Main Course   ○ Dessert   ○ Baking

Servings: .... Prep Time: .... Cook Time: ....

Difficulty: ○   ○   ○   ○   ○

Ingredients

....

....

....

....

....

....

....

....

....

Personal Notes:

Directions:

Rating:

Personal Notes:

17 Name:

Date: .... Source: ....

○ Starter   ○ Main Course   ○ Dessert   ○ Baking

Servings: .... Prep Time: .... Cook Time: ....

Difficulty: ○   ○   ○   ○   ○

Ingredients

....

....

....

....

....

....

....

....

....

Personal Notes:

Directions:

....

....

....

....

....

....

....

....

....

....

Rating:

Personal Notes:

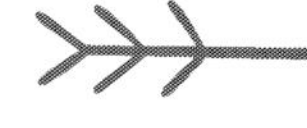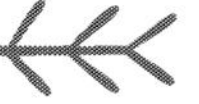

18 **Name:**
....

Date: .... Source: ....

○ Starter ○ Main Course ○ Dessert ○ Baking

Servings: .... Prep Time: .... Cook Time: ....

Difficulty: ○ ○ ○ ○ ○

Ingredients

....

....

....

....

....

....

....

....

....

Personal Notes:

Directions:

Rating: 

Personal Notes:

19 **Name:**

Date: .... Source: ....

○ Starter ○ Main Course ○ Dessert ○ Baking

Servings: .... Prep Time: .... Cook Time: ....

Difficulty: ○ ○ ○ ○ ○

Ingredients

....

....

....

....

....

....

....

....

....

Personal Notes:

Directions:

Rating: ☐ ☐ ☐ ☐ ☐

Personal Notes:

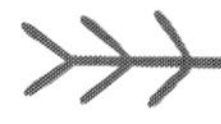

20 Name:

Date: Source:

◯ Starter   ◯ Main Course   ◯ Dessert   ◯ Baking

Servings: Prep Time: Cook Time:

Difficulty: ◯   ◯   ◯   ◯   ◯

Ingredients

Personal Notes:

Directions:

Rating: 🎩 🎩 🎩 🎩 🎩

Personal Notes:

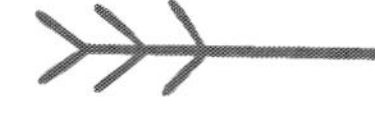

21 **Name:**

Date: Source:

○ Starter   ○ Main Course   ○ Dessert   ○ Baking

Servings: .... Prep Time: .... Cook Time: ....

Difficulty: ○ ○ ○ ○ ○

Ingredients

Personal Notes:

Directions:

Rating:

Personal Notes:

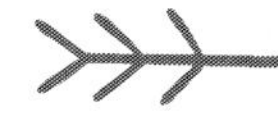

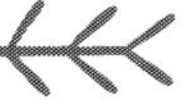

22 Name:

Date: Source:

○ Starter   ○ Main Course   ○ Dessert   ○ Baking

Servings: Prep Time: Cook Time:

Difficulty: ○   ○   ○   ○   ○

Ingredients

Personal Notes:

Rating:

Personal Notes:

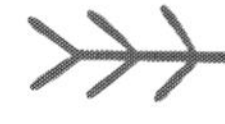

23

Name:

Date: Source:

◯ Starter   ◯ Main Course   ◯ Dessert   ◯ Baking

Servings: Prep Time: Cook Time:

Difficulty: ◯   ◯   ◯   ◯   ◯

Ingredients

Personal Notes:

Directions:

....

....

....

....

....

....

....

....

....

....

Rating:

Personal Notes:

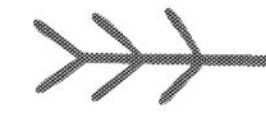

24 Name: ....

Date: .... Source: ....

◯ Starter ◯ Main Course ◯ Dessert ◯ Baking

Servings: .... Prep Time: .... Cook Time: ....

Difficulty: ◯ ◯ ◯ ◯ ◯

Ingredients

....

....

....

....

....

....

....

....

....

Personal Notes:

Directions:

Rating: 🧑‍🍳 🧑‍🍳 🧑‍🍳 🧑‍🍳 🧑‍🍳

Personal Notes:

25 Name:

Date: Source:

◯ Starter ◯ Main Course ◯ Dessert ◯ Baking

Servings: Prep Time: Cook Time:

Difficulty: ◯ ◯ ◯ ◯ ◯

Ingredients

Personal Notes:

Directions:

Rating: 

Personal Notes:

26 Name:

Date: .... Source: ....

○ Starter   ○ Main Course   ○ Dessert   ○ Baking

Servings: .... Prep Time: .... Cook Time: ....

Difficulty: ○   ○   ○   ○   ○

Ingredients

Personal Notes:

Directions:

Rating: 

Personal Notes:

27 Name:

Date: Source:

◯ Starter   ◯ Main Course   ◯ Dessert   ◯ Baking

Servings: Prep Time: Cook Time:

Difficulty: ◯   ◯   ◯   ◯   ◯

Ingredients

Personal Notes:

Directions:

Rating:

Personal Notes:

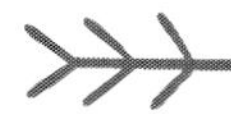 

28 Name:

Date: Source:

○ Starter   ○ Main Course   ○ Dessert   ○ Baking

Servings: Prep Time: Cook Time:

Difficulty: ○ ○ ○ ○ ○

Ingredients

Personal Notes:

Directions:

Rating:

Personal Notes:

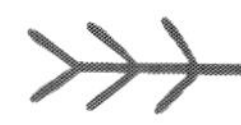

29 Name:

Date: Source:

○ Starter   ○ Main Course   ○ Dessert   ○ Baking

Servings: Prep Time: Cook Time:

Difficulty: ○   ○   ○   ○   ○

Ingredients

Personal Notes:

Directions:

Rating:  ♙ ♙ ♙ ♙ ♙

Personal Notes:

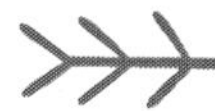

30 Name: ....

Date: .... Source: ....

◯ Starter   ◯ Main Course   ◯ Dessert   ◯ Baking

Servings: .... Prep Time: .... Cook Time: ....

Difficulty: ◯   ◯   ◯   ◯   ◯

Ingredients

....

....

....

....

....

....

....

....

Personal Notes:

Directions:

Rating: ☐ ☐ ☐ ☐ ☐

Personal Notes:

31

Name:

Date: .... Source: ....

○ Starter   ○ Main Course   ○ Dessert   ○ Baking

Servings: .... Prep Time: .... Cook Time: ....

Difficulty: ○   ○   ○   ○   ○

Ingredients

Personal Notes:

Directions:

....

....

....

....

....

....

....

....

....

....

Rating: ☐ ☐ ☐ ☐ ☐

Personal Notes:

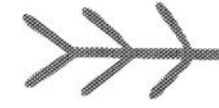

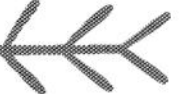

32

Name:
....

Date: .... Source: ....

○ Starter   ○ Main Course   ○ Dessert   ○ Baking

Servings: .... Prep Time: .... Cook Time: ....

Difficulty: ○   ○   ○   ○   ○

Ingredients

....

....

....

....

....

....

....

....

....

Personal Notes:

Directions:

Rating: 🧑‍🍳 🧑‍🍳 🧑‍🍳 🧑‍🍳 🧑‍🍳

Personal Notes:

33 Name:

Date: .... Source: ....

○ Starter　○ Main Course　○ Dessert　○ Baking

Servings: .... Prep Time: .... Cook Time: ....

Difficulty: ○　○　○　○　○

Ingredients

....

....

....

....

....

....

....

....

....

Personal Notes:

Directions:

Rating:

Personal Notes:

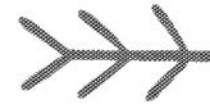 

Name: ....

Date: .... **Source:** ....

○ Starter   ○ Main Course   ○ Dessert   ○ Baking

Servings: .... **Prep Time:** .... **Cook Time:** ....

Difficulty: ○   ○   ○   ○   ○

Ingredients

....

....

....

....

....

....

....

....

....

Personal Notes:

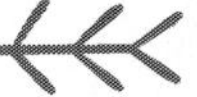

Directions:

Rating: 🍳 🍳 🍳 🍳 🍳

Personal Notes:

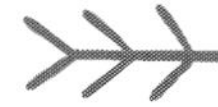 

Name:
....

Date: .... Source: ....

○ Starter   ○ Main Course   ○ Dessert   ○ Baking

Servings: .... Prep Time: .... Cook Time: ....

Difficulty: ○   ○   ○   ○   ○

Ingredients

....

....

....

....

....

....

....

....

....

Personal Notes:

Directions:

Rating: 🧑‍🍳 🧑‍🍳 🧑‍🍳 🧑‍🍳 🧑‍🍳

Personal Notes:

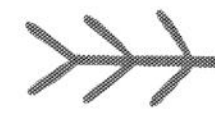

36 Name:

Date: Source:

◯ Starter   ◯ Main Course   ◯ Dessert   ◯ Baking

Servings: Prep Time: Cook Time:

Difficulty: ◯   ◯   ◯   ◯   ◯

Ingredients

Personal Notes:

Directions:

....

....

....

....

....

....

....

....

....

....

....

Rating:

Personal Notes:

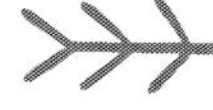

83

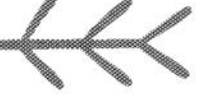

37 Name:

Date: Source:

○ Starter   ○ Main Course   ○ Dessert   ○ Baking

Servings: Prep Time: Cook Time:

Difficulty: ○   ○   ○   ○   ○

Ingredients

Personal Notes:

Directions:

....

....

....

....

....

....

....

....

....

....

....

....

Rating:

Personal Notes:

Name: ....

Date: .... Source: ....

○ Starter   ○ Main Course   ○ Dessert   ○ Baking

Servings: .... Prep Time: .... Cook Time: ....

Difficulty: ○   ○   ○   ○   ○

Ingredients

....

....

....

....

....

....

....

....

....

Personal Notes:

Directions:

Rating: 

Personal Notes:

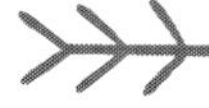

39   Name:

Date: ....   Source: ....

○ Starter   ○ Main Course   ○ Dessert   ○ Baking

Servings: ....   Prep Time: ....   Cook Time: ....

Difficulty: ○   ○   ○   ○   ○

Ingredients

....

....

....

....

....

....

....

....

....

Personal Notes:

Directions:

....

....

....

....

....

....

....

....

....

....

....

Rating:

Personal Notes:

40 Name:

Date: .... Source: ....

○ Starter   ○ Main Course   ○ Dessert   ○ Baking

Servings: .... Prep Time: .... Cook Time: ....

Difficulty: ○   ○   ○   ○   ○

Ingredients

....

....

....

....

....

....

....

....

....

Personal Notes:

Directions:

Rating: 

Personal Notes:

41

Name:

Date: .... Source: ....

○ Starter ○ Main Course ○ Dessert ○ Baking

Servings: .... Prep Time: .... Cook Time: ....

Difficulty: ○ ○ ○ ○ ○

Ingredients

....

....

....

....

....

....

....

....

Personal Notes:

Directions:

Rating: ♟ ♟ ♟ ♟ ♟

Personal Notes:

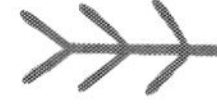

Name:

Date: Source:

○ Starter   ○ Main Course   ○ Dessert   ○ Baking

Servings: Prep Time: Cook Time:

Difficulty: ○   ○   ○   ○   ○

Ingredients

Personal Notes:

Directions:

Rating: 

Personal Notes:

43 Name:

Date: .... Source: ....

○ Starter ○ Main Course ○ Dessert ○ Baking

Servings: .... Prep Time: .... Cook Time: ....

Difficulty: ○ ○ ○ ○ ○

Ingredients

....

....

....

....

....

....

....

....

....

Personal Notes:

Directions:

Rating: ☐ ☐ ☐ ☐ ☐

Personal Notes:

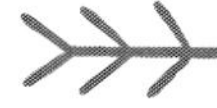

44 Name: ....

Date: .... Source: ....

○ Starter ○ Main Course ○ Dessert ○ Baking

Servings: .... Prep Time: .... Cook Time: ....

Difficulty: ○ ○ ○ ○ ○

Ingredients

....

....

....

....

....

....

....

....

....

Personal Notes:

Directions:

Rating: 

Personal Notes:

Name:

Date: Source:

○ Starter   ○ Main Course   ○ Dessert   ○ Baking

Servings: Prep Time: Cook Time:

Difficulty: ○   ○   ○   ○   ○

Ingredients

Personal Notes:

Directions:

....

....

....

....

....

....

....

....

....

....

....

....

Rating:

Personal Notes:

Name:

Date: Source:

○ Starter   ○ Main Course   ○ Dessert   ○ Baking

Servings: Prep Time: Cook Time:

Difficulty: ○   ○   ○   ○   ○

Ingredients

Personal Notes:

Directions:

Rating: ♙ ♙ ♙ ♙ ♙

Personal Notes:

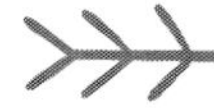

47

Name: ....

Date: .... Source: ....

○ Starter   ○ Main Course   ○ Dessert   ○ Baking

Servings: .... Prep Time: .... Cook Time: ....

Difficulty: ○   ○   ○   ○   ○

Ingredients

....

....

....

....

....

....

....

....

Personal Notes:

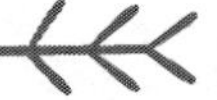

Directions:

Rating: 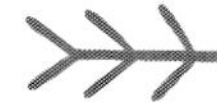

Personal Notes:

48 Name:

Date: .... Source: ....

○ Starter ○ Main Course ○ Dessert ○ Baking

Servings: .... Prep Time: .... Cook Time: ....

Difficulty: ○ ○ ○ ○ ○

Ingredients

....

....

....

....

....

....

....

....

....

Personal Notes:

Directions:

Rating:

Personal Notes:

49 Name:

Date: Source:

○ Starter   ○ Main Course   ○ Dessert   ○ Baking

Servings: Prep Time: Cook Time:

Difficulty: ○   ○   ○   ○   ○

Ingredients

Personal Notes:

Directions:

Rating: 🎩 🎩 🎩 🎩 🎩

Personal Notes:

50 Name:

Date: .... Source: ....

○ Starter ○ Main Course ○ Dessert ○ Baking

Servings: .... Prep Time: .... Cook Time: ....

Difficulty: ○ ○ ○ ○ ○

Ingredients

....

....

....

....

....

....

....

....

....

Personal Notes:

Directions:

Rating: 

Personal Notes:

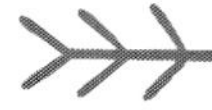

51

Name:
....

Date: .... Source: ....

○ Starter   ○ Main Course   ○ Dessert   ○ Baking

Servings: .... Prep Time: .... Cook Time: ....

Difficulty: ○   ○   ○   ○   ○

Ingredients

....

....

....

....

....

....

....

....

Personal Notes:

Directions:

....

....

....

....

....

....

....

....

....

....

Rating:

Personal Notes:

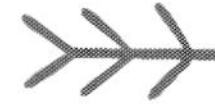

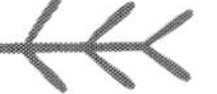

52 Name:

Date: Source:

○ Starter   ○ Main Course   ○ Dessert   ○ Baking

Servings: Prep Time: Cook Time:

Difficulty: ○   ○   ○   ○   ○

Ingredients

Personal Notes:

Directions:

Rating:

Personal Notes:

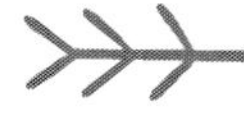

Name:

Date: Source:

○ Starter   ○ Main Course   ○ Dessert   ○ Baking

Servings: Prep Time: Cook Time:

Difficulty: ○   ○   ○   ○   ○

Ingredients

Personal Notes:

Directions:

....

....

....

....

....

....

....

....

....

....

....

Rating:

Personal Notes:

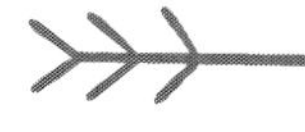

54 Name:

Date: .... Source: ....

○ Starter ○ Main Course ○ Dessert ○ Baking

Servings: .... Prep Time: .... Cook Time: ....

Difficulty: ○ ○ ○ ○ ○

Ingredients

....

....

....

....

....

....

....

....

....

Personal Notes:

Directions:

Rating: 🍳 🍳 🍳 🍳 🍳

Personal Notes:

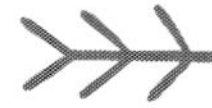

55 Name: ....

Date: .... Source: ....

○ Starter   ○ Main Course   ○ Dessert   ○ Baking

Servings: .... Prep Time: .... Cook Time: ....

Difficulty: ○   ○   ○   ○   ○

Ingredients

....

....

....

....

....

....

....

....

Personal Notes:

Directions:

Rating: ♢ ♢ ♢ ♢ ♢

Personal Notes:

56 Name:

Date: Source:

○ Starter ○ Main Course ○ Dessert ○ Baking

Servings: Prep Time: Cook Time:

Difficulty: ○ ○ ○ ○ ○

Ingredients

Personal Notes:

Directions:

....

....

....

....

....

....

....

....

....

....

Rating:

Personal Notes:

57 Name:

Date: .... Source: ....

○ Starter ○ Main Course ○ Dessert ○ Baking

Servings: .... Prep Time: .... Cook Time: ....

Difficulty: ○ ○ ○ ○ ○

Ingredients

....

....

....

....

....

....

....

....

....

Personal Notes:

Directions:

Rating:

Personal Notes:

58 Name:

Date: .... Source: ....

○ Starter ○ Main Course ○ Dessert ○ Baking

Servings: .... Prep Time: .... Cook Time: ....

Difficulty: ○ ○ ○ ○ ○

Ingredients

....

....

....

....

....

....

....

....

Personal Notes:

Directions:

Rating: ☐ ☐ ☐ ☐ ☐

Personal Notes:

59 Name:

Date: Source:

○ Starter   ○ Main Course   ○ Dessert   ○ Baking

Servings: Prep Time: Cook Time:

Difficulty: ○   ○   ○   ○   ○

Ingredients

Personal Notes:

Directions:

....

....

....

....

....

....

....

....

....

....

....

Rating:

Personal Notes:

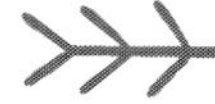

60 **Name:**
....

Date: .... Source: ....

◯ Starter   ◯ Main Course   ◯ Dessert   ◯ Baking

Servings: .... Prep Time: .... Cook Time: ....

Difficulty: ◯   ◯   ◯   ◯   ◯

Ingredients

....

....

....

....

....

....

....

....

Personal Notes:

Directions:

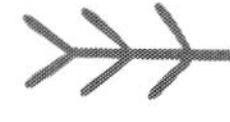

Rating: 🧑‍🍳 🧑‍🍳 🧑‍🍳 🧑‍🍳 🧑‍🍳

Personal Notes:

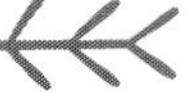

61 Name:

Date: ....   Source: ....

○ Starter   ○ Main Course   ○ Dessert   ○ Baking

Servings: ....   Prep Time: ....   Cook Time: ....

Difficulty: ○   ○   ○   ○   ○

Ingredients

....

....

....

....

....

....

....

....

Personal Notes:

Directions:

Rating: ☐ ☐ ☐ ☐ ☐

Personal Notes:

Name:

Date: Source:

○ Starter   ○ Main Course   ○ Dessert   ○ Baking

Servings: Prep Time: Cook Time:

Difficulty: ○   ○   ○   ○   ○

Ingredients

Personal Notes:

Directions:

Rating: 🍳 🍳 🍳 🍳 🍳

Personal Notes:

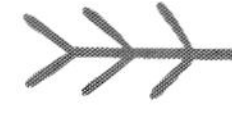 

63 **Name:**
....

Date: .... Source: ....

◯ Starter   ◯ Main Course   ◯ Dessert   ◯ Baking

Servings: .... Prep Time: .... Cook Time: ....

Difficulty: ◯   ◯   ◯   ◯   ◯

Ingredients

....

....

....

....

....

....

....

....

Personal Notes:

Directions:

Rating: 

Personal Notes:

64 Name:

Date: .... Source: ....

○ Starter ○ Main Course ○ Dessert ○ Baking

Servings: .... Prep Time: .... Cook Time: ....

Difficulty: ○ ○ ○ ○ ○

Ingredients

....

....

....

....

....

....

....

....

....

Personal Notes:

Directions:

....

....

....

....

....

....

....

....

....

....

....

....

Rating:

Personal Notes:

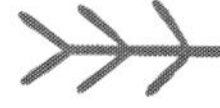

Made in the USA
Monee, IL
07 July 2026